Cheer and Groan

John Townsend

Stanley Thornes (Publishers) Ltd

Originally published 1985 by Hutchinson Education
Reprinted 1985, 1986, 1988

Reprinted 1992 by
Stanley Thornes (Publishers) Ltd
Ellenborough House
Wellington Street
CHELTENHAM GL50 1YD
England

Reprinted 1994, 1995

British Library Cataloguing in Publication Data

Townsend, John, 1924–
    Cheer and groan. — (Spirals).
    1. Readers – 1950 –
    I. Title   II. Series
    428.6   PE1119

    ISBN 0 7487 1063 9

Printed and bound in Great Britain by
Martin's The Printers, Berwick.

Contents

Note: Cards saying 'BOO', 'HISS', 'CHEER', 'GROAN'
etc. will be of great use during both plays, so that
the appropriate sound can be made by the audience.
Much overacting is also called for.

A complete list of Spirals

Stories

Jim Alderson
Crash in the Jungle
The Witch Princess

Jan Carew
Death Comes to the Circus

Susan Duberley
The Ring

**Keith Fletcher and
Susan Duberley**
Nightmare Lake

John Goodwin
Dead-end Job

Paul Groves
Not that I'm Work-shy
The Third Climber

Anita Jackson
The Actor
The Austin Seven
Bennet Manor
Dreams
The Ear
A Game of Life or Death
No Rent to Pay

Paul Jennings
Eye of Evil
Maggot

Margaret Loxton
The Dark Shadow

Patrick Nobes
Ghost Writer

Kevin Philbin
Summer of the Werewolf

John Townsend
Beware of the Morris Minor
Fame and Fortune
SOS

David Walke
Dollars in the Dust

Plays

Jan Carew
Computer Killer
No Entry
Time Loop

John Godfrey
When I Count to Three

Nigel Gray
An Earwig in the Ear

Paul Groves
Tell Me Where it Hurts

Barbara Mitchelhill
Punchlines
The Ramsbottoms at Home

Madeline Sotheby
Hard Times at Batwing Hall

John Townsend
Cheer and Groan
The End of the Line
Hanging by a Fred
The Lighthouse Keeper's Secret
Making a Splash
Murder at Muckleby Manor
Over and Out
Rocking the Boat
Taking the Plunge

David Walke
The Bungle Gang Strikes Again
The Good, the Bad and the Bungle
Package Holiday

Boo and Hiss

4 parts:
Jenny
George, her wet husband
Sir Vile Pits, the evil landlord
Sidney, the long-lost brother

Scene: A slum of the worst kind. It is a dark room with just one chair, a cot (with a baby in it) and a door.

Jenny	[*Almost crying*] Oh, George.
George	I know.
Jenny	Oh, George.
George	I know.
Jenny	Our baby is so pale. We have had nothing to eat for days.
George	I know.
Jenny	This hole where we live is so damp. I am so cold. We are all ill. There is not a crumb of food in the room. We don't even have a bed.

George	I know.
Jenny	This slum is so dirty.
George	I know.
Jenny	And freezing. There is ice on the walls, frost on the floor and icicles on the baby.
George	I know.
Jenny	But George, what are we to do? Sir Vile Pits is coming today to collect our rent. We don't have a penny.
George	I know.
Jenny	Then what the dash are you going to do about it?
George	I don't really know.
Jenny	Oh, George! [*In floods of tears*] You must find a job. [*SNIFF!*] You must earn some money before we all starve. You must bring back some pennies to our hole – before we have to beg in the streets, before we have to chop up this chair for firewood, before we have to set light to the baby's cot to thaw him out, before we are all thrown out into the ice and snow – before we, yes, George, before we all DIE!

George	It does look rather grim, doesn't it?
Jenny	Is that all you can say? Don't you realize what it's like for me being locked up here all day – just me and our child?
George	Well, I'm here as well.
Jenny	But you shouldn't be. You should be working.
George	[*Looking startled*] Working?
Jenny	We can't last much longer.
George	Oh, I know.
Jenny	Please don't start all that again. Oh, George, for our baby's sake – please go now and don't come home till you find a crust.
George	You mean....
Jenny	Yes, George. Get some bread for us to eat and stop loafing around.
George	I'll try, Jenny, my dear, my love, my pet, my poppet, my ... gosh! The baker's is miles away. I'll have to *walk*! Besides, they'll want MONEY.
Jenny	Then earn some, George – please! Bring back some pennies to your starving wife and child.

George	I'll do what I can. I'm sorry I've let you down. [*He begins to cry*] I'm sorry I'm no good to you. Oh, forgive me.
Jenny	Don't say that, George. Dear George. Never say that. Why, you're such a good man in other ways.
George	Oh Jenny, do you really mean that?
Jenny	Er well yes.
George	You're a fine woman, Jenny. [*They hug*] [*CHEER!*]
Jenny	Oh, George.
George	Oh, Jenny.
Jenny	Oh, George.
George	Oh, Jenny.
	[*Baby burps in cot*] [*OOPS!*]
Both	Oh, dear!
Jenny	Nothing must ever come between us.
George	You're right, Jenny. I must be a man. I'll do what I can. [*Puts on hat*] I will search the streets to find a job. I will call at every factory, every house, every shop until I find work. Yes, Jenny, you

can rely on me. I will not fail you or let you down. [*He leaves*] [*CHEER!*]

Jenny [*Sinking to her knees*] Every day is the same. My poor George can never find work. We will never have the money to buy food, clothes, coal or to pay the rent. What can I do? My whole life has been full of tears. I have never known what a happy home life is like – not since my poor twin brother went away ... Sidney. He went off to Africa to find his fortune. He was a game hunter, but ooh! [*Sobs*] It was so sad. Only last week I heard the news. He was eaten by a lion in the jungle. Poor Sidney. The beast knocked him off his bike and ate him up. It's put me off Meals on Wheels for life. But hark, I hear someone outside. [*Loud knocking*] Who can it be at this hour? Can it be my George so soon? Perhaps he has found money at last!

[*Opens door and in barges* Sir Vile Pits] [*BOO!*]

Sir Pits Ha ha ha. What, all alone?

Jenny Why, yes. Just me and little Gale.

Sir Pits	Gale? Gale? Who on earth is Gale?
Jenny	My little baby.
Sir Pits	Gale? Gale? Why the heck did you call it Gale?
Jenny	Well, she has such dreadful wind, you see.
Sir Pits	Bah! I couldn't care less about you or your weedy kid. Can't you guess what I want?
Jenny	Oh no! Not....
Sir Pits	Yes....
Jenny	You mean....
Sir Pits	THE RENT.
Jenny	But what am I to do?
Sir Pits	Are you trying to tell me something?
Jenny	Um. Mmmm. Yes.
Sir Pits	What?
Jenny	Well....
Sir Pits	[Grabs her] Eh? [*HISS!*]
Jenny	Oh, no!
Sir Pits	Ooh, yes.

Jenny	Please.
Sir Pits	Now.
Jenny	What?
Sir Pits	Rent.
Jenny	Oh.
Sir Pits	Yes.
Jenny	How?
Sir Pits	What?
Jenny	Where?
Sir Pits	Here.
Jenny	When?
Sir Pits	NOW! Where is my money?
Jenny	It's ... it's ... oh! I can hide it from you no longer.
Sir Pits	You mean to say....
Jenny	Yes, I don't have it yet, but I will. Really. Oh believe me, Sir Pits. I shall do my best. My George is doing what he can at this very moment. Isn't that enough?
Sir Pits	[*Hits her*] [*BOO!*] Bah, what is the good of that? My rent is due and I will make

	sure I will get it. You will be thrown out into the streets for all I care. You and your ugly little brat—out, out, OUT into the gutter. You will rot in prison for this – just you see, ha ha ha!
Jenny	Oh please, have pity on me.
Sir Pits	Why should I? There is one thing you could do to make things better.
Jenny	Oh yes, please. Let me do something for you.
Sir Pits	How about giving your kind landlord a nice kiss?
Jenny	No, please.
Sir Pits	Oh, go on. Make an old man happy.
Jenny	No. No.
Sir Pits	I insist.
Jenny	No. No.
Sir Pits	How dare you say no. Why? Why won't you kiss me?
Jenny	Because. . . .
Sir Pits	Yes? Why is it?
Jenny	You're vile.
Sir Pits	Any other reason?

Jenny	Yes. I hate you.
Sir Pits	Is that all? Oh come on, my dear. You must like me really. Let me take you away from here. Let me sweep you off your feet like the waves on the shore.
Jenny	Waves on the shore?
Sir Pits	Yes, the sea, Jenny, the sea. Aren't I like the power of the great sea? Don't I remind you of the sea, eh, Jenny?
Jenny	In a way.
Sir Pits	Ah ha, now we're getting somewhere. Is it because it's so strong, wild and deep?
Jenny	No. It's wet, it smells and it makes me sick. [*CHEER!*]
Sir Pits	Bah! You will regret those cruel words. You've done it now. I will return in one hour. If my money is not here then, I will crush you like a worm under my boot, I will chew you up and spit you out, I will tear you apart with my own bare hands and throw little bits of you out into the snow. Do I make myself quite clear?
Jenny	Sort of.
Sir Pits	Good. Then we know where we stand,

don't we? Ha ha, or in your case, where you will lie – the gutter! Ha ha, I will be back within the hour. Just you see! [*He storms out*] [*BOO* and *HISS*]

Jenny

[*Weeping on the floor*] No, oh no. Please, oh no. My child is so weak. I am so unhappy. Where is George to hold my hand? All is lost – LOST. Oh no, what can I do? [*Knock at door*] I must kill myself. I will plunge a knife into my broken heart. Who can it be at the door? Surely Sir Pits hasn't come back so soon. Oh please, Sir Pits, have pity on a helpless girl. Don't hit me again. Give me time.

[*The door opens and a head pops round. It is* Sidney. *He is dressed in shorts and cycle clips. He carries a polo stick. He has come straight from the jungle*]

Sidney

Oh, I say.

Jenny

Please leave me. Go and leave me to my doom.

Sidney

Well I never!

Jenny

There is nothing left for me to do.

Sidney

A cup of tea would be nice.

Jenny	Wait. That voice. Who can it be? [*She looks up*]
Sidney	It is me.
Jenny	It can't be!
Sidney	Well it jolly well is.
Jenny	You mean ... is it...?
Sidney	Sidney.
Jenny	Sidney! [*CHEER!*]
Sidney	Your long-lost twin brother. [*They kiss*]
Jenny	It can't be true. Where have you been?
Sidney	I've just come back from the bush.
Jenny	The gooseberry bush? You've been up the garden all this time?
Sidney	No – the jungle, silly!
Jenny	But I heard that a lion killed you.
Sidney	It was a dashed near thing.
Jenny	Were you hurt?
Sidney	Just scratched.
Jenny	Where did it get you?
Sidney	Right in the middle of the Congo. It's all right. I hit it with my polo stick and then shot it.

Jenny	The lion?
Sidney	No, the polo stick.
Jenny	You play polo?
Sidney	Oh yes, all the time now. It's the game of kings, princes and the jolly well-off. [*GOSH!*]
Jenny	Oh Sidney, I can't believe you're here. You have made my day. I am so happy. But what will you do now?
Sidney	Oh didn't I tell you?
Jenny	Tell me? Tell me what?
Sidney	I'm rolling in it.
Jenny	Rolling in it?
Sidney	Yes, rolling in it.
Jenny	Is that what the smell is? I thought it was the drains.
Sidney	No, no. I'm filthy rich.
Jenny	You made your fortune after all?
Sidney	And more. I work in fur coats now.
Jenny	That must be a jolly warm job. Do they fit you?
Sidney	No, Jenny. I make them – from animal skins. I've made a lot of money and so

	I've come to take you away from this awful hole.
Jenny	And George?
Sidney	You want me to take you away from him as well?
Jenny	No, no. Do you have enough money for him too?
Sidney	I've got pots of the stuff. Look. [*Takes out purse*] That's just a spot. I plan to work on the railways next.
Jenny	You want to drive trains?
Sidney	Oh, no. To own them.
Jenny	How super.
Sidney	But why were you crying just then?
Jenny	It was the landlord.
Sidney	Oh, I could have sworn it was you.
Jenny	No. The cruel man was about to throw us out into the street where we would starve.
Sidney	Who is this evil wretch?
	[Sir Pits *suddenly bursts in* [HISS]
Sir Pits	Sir Vile Pits! I'm here to do my deed. Your hour is up.

Jenny	No, please.
Sir Pits	I will rip you up, limb from limb. I will beat you black and blue. I will rob you of all you own – not a fat lot, but I'll take it all the same. [*BOO*] Wait a minute – who is this silly little worm?
Jenny	Sidney.
Sidney	How dare you!
Sir Pits	Out my way, you toad.
Sidney	Do you know who I am?
Sir Pits	Yes. A feeble weed. Now get out of here before I pull you up and toss you on the compost heap.
Sidney	But I'm rolling in it.
Sir Pits	You certainly will be.
Sidney	You can't talk to me like that. I'm a big game hunter.
Sir Pits	More like a short fat fibber.
Sidney	I didn't come here to be insulted.
Sir Pits	Oh no? So where do you normally go?
Sidney	Look, I'm telling you, I shoot animals.
Sir Pits	[*Thumps him*] Prove it.

Sidney	Very well. [*Takes gun from pocket and shoots*] [*CHEER!*]
Sir Pits	Ouch! Ah, my arm. Why? I'm no animal.
Sidney	Oh yes, you are.
Sir Pits	Oh no, I'm not.
Jenny	Oh yes, you are.
Sir Pits	Oh no, I'm not.
Sidney	Now, get out of here and leave my sister alone before I shoot you between the eyes.
Sir Pits	You wouldn't dare – would you?
Jenny	He killed a wild lion last week.
Sir Pits	How do you know it was wild?
Sidney	Well it certainly wasn't very pleased about it. And I'll do the same to you, you crook.
Sir Pits	But this lion – what did you have to do to it then?
Sidney	Stuff it.
Sir Pits	I'm sorry I asked.
Sidney	Here – take the money owed to you. [*Throws him the purse*] Now get out of this hole for good. Go, and never come

back, or your head will be stuck up on the wall next to the lion, above my fireplace for all to see.

Sir Pits   I will. I shall go. Spare me. Don't shoot again, please. Have mercy, I will never come back, I promise. [*He leaves*] [*CHEER!*]

Jenny   Oh, Sidney, you were wonderful. What would I have done without you? Look, my baby is smiling. She hasn't done that before. Please take us away from here and we can all be happy for ever. All my worries are over. They will never come back.

[George *bursts in, grinning*]

George   I've got it.

Jenny   We know, George, but you'll get over it.

George   No, a job at the railway station.

Jenny   What as?

George   A handyman.

Jenny   But you can't work with your hands. You've never been any good at that sort of thing. Oh, George, why on earth did you tell them you're a handyman?

George	Because I live only just round the corner. That's very handy. [*GROAN!*]
Sidney	You can come and work for me.
George	Good grief ... Sidney! I thought you were ... you know, er well, sort of um ... dead.
Jenny	He's rich, George. He plays polo with the well-off.
Sidney	I'm dead rich! I'm now going to take you all away from here.
George	Golly!
Sidney	It's funny that you should get a job on the railway, George. I have, too.
George	You mean you are going to work on the trains as well?
Sidney	You're on the right lines. [*GROAN!*] I will own them, so you were close. You were certainly on the right track. [*GROAN!*]
George	First class!
Jenny	And we will never see Sir Vile Pits again!
Sidney	You can come and watch me play polo right now. I have a match with a duke.
George	Oh rather, we'd love to. Good show! Oh

	Jenny, I knew all along it would all work out in the end.
Jenny	Oh, George, you are such a fine man.
George	I suppose you're right.
Sidney	Come on. We shall all live happily together. All your bad times have blown away with the wind.

[*Baby burps again*] [*OOPS!*]

Come with me now to polo and leave this awful hole. All my cash is now yours. We have a mint of money between us.

Jenny	I am so happy, George, MY George.
George	I know.
Jenny	Isn't it super?
George	I know. But now it's POLO time. We'll leave this HOLE WITH A MINT – at last!

[*They all exit to GROAN!*]

Cheer and Groan

4 parts:
Bertie
Lucy
Sinbad Sneer
Basil Brimwick

Scene: A shabby upstairs room which is *Lucy's* home.

Bertie   Gin. I must have a drop of gin. Where can I find gin? I want it. I need it. I love it. I'll die for it. I'll KILL for it! I drink to live – I live to drink. Yes, gin is all I live for now. It is my only hope. I've got to find some. But where is it? I have none left. I have no money. That is why I have come here. Dear Lucy must be able to help. Yes, without gin, what can I do?

[Lucy *enters*]

Lucy   Hello, Bertie. Have you come to take me out for the evening? Have you come to bring me a birthday present? Have you come to treat me to a meal?

Bertie	Not really.
Lucy	Ooh, is it a surprise? How sweet of you, Bertie. I do like a surprise. Then what have you come for?
Bertie	I'll give you a clue. I need something starting with a 'G' and ending in 'N'.
Lucy	But why do you want a gun?
Bertie	No. No. 'T', not 'U'.
Lucy	You not me? What do you mean, you not me?
Bertie	Gun. Put 'T'. Get rid of 'U'.
Lucy	Gun? Get rid of me? You're not going to shoot me, are you, Bertie?
Bertie	I'll give you another clue. I take a full one to bed every night to warm my throat and help me to sleep.
Lucy	A hot water bottle?
Bertie	I need a drink, Lucy. Something good and soothing, something I need for strength, for peace of mind, for LIFE! [*GASP!*]
Lucy	Oh, of course. Help yourself. There's some milk in the jug.
Bertie	No. Oh Lucy, no. Can't you think? Can't

	you guess? Can't you understand what I live for?
Lucy	Me?
Bertie	Oh Lucy, I must tell you the truth. I can't hide it from you any more. I have come here for....
Lucy	For what?
Bertie	Well....
Lucy	Yes?
Bertie	Er um.
Lucy	Spit it out.
Bertie	I couldn't do that.
Lucy	Why?
Bertie	I love it so much.
Lucy	Do you mean...?
Bertie	I think I do. You see, Lucy – MY Lucy, I have no money. I have spent it all on that thing I need for life. I go miles for it. I always come home with it.
Lucy	The bus?
Bertie	No. Gin.
Lucy	Much?

Bertie	Yes.
Lucy	Often?
Bertie	Yes.
Lucy	Where?
Bertie	Here.
Lucy	Here?
Bertie	There.
Lucy	Where?
Bertie	Everywhere.
Lucy	But I have no gin.
Bertie	Surely you must have a drop.
Lucy	None.
Bertie	Please.
Lucy	It's gone.
Bertie	Gone?
Lucy	Gone.
Bertie	Lucy, I'm a thirsty man.
Lucy	There is water in the tap.
Bertie	Don't I make myself clear? A thirsty man is an angry man.

Lucy	Oh dear.
Bertie	If I don't have gin I will have to end it all. I will throw myself into the sea, taking with me the only thing that means anything to me any more.
Lucy	You'd take me with you?
Bertie	Not you, a bottle of gin. I could leap from the cliffs with a bottle in my hands. You know what they'd call it, don't you?
Lucy	Gin on the rocks?
Bertie	Suicide, Lucy. That's what it would be. I will end it all if you don't give me gin. [*GULP!*]
Lucy	You mean you didn't really come here to see me at all?
Bertie	Er ... of course.
Lucy	You haven't come to take me out for a birthday treat?
Bertie	Er well ...
Lucy	It's only my gin you want, isn't it? [*Sobs*] I am upset, Bertie. You said we were going out.
Bertie	Did I?
Lucy	Yes.

Bertie	When?
Lucy	Last week. You promised. Oh Bertie – I am going up to change into my best dress and when I come back, we'll forget all this upset and go and spend a nice evening out. Do you hear? [*She leaves*]
Bertie	At last! I am alone in this room. I'll search it high and low. There must be money here. Then I can buy gin. Yes, I must have gin. [*HISS! As he searches room*] All I need are a few coins and I can be a happy man again. Aha! What can be in this tin? Cash! At last, some pennies for my gin. In the tax tin. Ten pence. I will take it all. [*BOO!*] She won't know if I take any. It's all I need. It's all I want. It's all she's got! I had better put something back inside the tin so it will still rattle and sound full. Yes, some nails, some tin tacks in the tax tin. Oh no, I can hear Lucy. She is coming back. I must go. I will creep out the back way. With this ten pence I can buy enough gin at the Queen's Arms to last me the night. Ha ha.

[*He exits one way as Lucy enters from the other*] [*CHEER!*]

Lucy	Bertie? Bertie? Where are you? Do you like my new dress? I have saved hard for weeks to buy it. I have worked overtime at the mill for so long – only to find I now have to pay extra tax. Never mind, I've just about saved enough and put it away in a safe place. The tax man will be round for my tax tin sometime. At last I've saved it all. But where is Bertie? Bertie, where have you gone? [*Knocking at door*] Oh, perhaps that's him at the door. He must have popped out. [*Opens door*] Hello, can I help you?
Sneer	[*Walking in*] I jolly well hope so.
Lucy	But who are you?
Sneer	Sinbad Sneer. *The* Sinbad Sneer. [*HISS!*]
Lucy	Not. . . .
Sneer	Yes – the tax man. [*BOO!*] You owe ten pence – and I want it all now.
Lucy	It's all right. I've put it all in a tin. I've saved it all up.
Sneer	Good. Then give it to me and I shall go. I would hate to send another poor soul to prison. Ha ha ha.
Lucy	Oh, I have all the money, Mr Sneer,

don't worry about that. It is over here. There you are, you can take my tax tin and keep it. You can hear it is full of money.

Sneer   Just a moment. Not so fast. You don't think I'm fool enough to take your word for it, do you? I must open it and count every penny.

Lucy   Isn't my word good enough?

Sneer   Your word? Your word? Who cares about your word? Now, out of my way. Let me count the money.

Lucy   Of course. You'll find it all there. You can trust me. [*GASP!*]

Sneer   [*Opening tin*] Bah! What's this? You've tried to trick me. You are under arrest for fraud. You are no more than a crook and a cheat. It's a crime to rob the tax man. There's not a penny here.

Lucy   There must be.

Sneer   Well there isn't.

Lucy   But I don't see how.

Sneer   I don't see anything.

Lucy   Look again. There must be tax in the tax tin.

Sneer	None. Just tin tacks.
Lucy	Tin tacks? Tin tacks? You mean to say there's not tax in the tax tin, just tin tacks in the tax tin?
Sneer	It's just a tin tacks tin with tin tacks in. All tin and no tax.
Lucy	Oh no, there are only tin tacks where the tax has been.
Sneer	I don't like your tricks with the tin tacks tax tin.
Lucy	I beg your pardon?
Sneer	Bah, stop all this tripe. I want the money.
Lucy	But if it's not in the tin, I don't have it. It has gone.
Sneer	Gone?
Lucy	Yes, gone. It was there a few minutes ago. Where could it have gone? Who could have ... oh no ... not Bertie?
Sneer	I am not leaving here till I get the money. I hope I make myself clear.
Lucy	But please believe me. It was here in my tax tin.
Sneer	Bah! [*He throws the tin out of the window*] What rot. Get rid of the tax tin.

I want ten pence and I mean to get it by hook or by crook – I don't mind which. [*HISS!*]

Lucy   You don't understand.

Sneer   I think I do. You tried to trick me. No one does that to Sinbad Sneer. No one makes a fool of me. No one, do you hear?

Lucy   Mmmm.

Sneer   No one tries to cheat a tax man – least of all me. If you don't pay up I will drag you through the streets to the workhouse where you will rot for years, ha ha ha. [*BOO!*]

Lucy   How horrid.

Sneer   And what is more.... [*Knock at the door*] Who is that?

Lucy   It could be Bertie. He could have my money.

Sneer   MY money. Then let him in at once.

Lucy   [*Opens door*] Hello?

Sneer   Who is it?

Lucy   I don't know.

Sneer   Send him away.

Lucy	I've never seen him before.
Basil	Is this your house, miss?
Lucy	Well, yes.
Sneer	Not for much longer.
Basil	I am Basil. May I come in?
Lucy	Yes.
Sneer	No.
Basil	Did you just throw a tin out of your window?
Lucy	Er well ....
Basil	A heavy tin that crashed onto the street below?
Sneer	It was her tax tin. It wasn't me. I didn't do it.
Lucy	But, but....
Basil	Showering sharp tin tacks in the road?
Lucy	Well, you see....
Sneer	Yes, it was her. She did it. Ha ha. Another crime to lock you away. Yes, I saw her do it.
Basil	Was it your tin, miss?
Basil	I'm afraid it was, but you see....

Basil	Then I must give you this.
Lucy	But why? It's a purse full of gold. [*CHEER!*]
Sneer	What?
Basil	You saved my life. [*GOSH!*]
Sneer	It was me, you fool.
Basil	I was down in the street, walking to the bank when two armed robbers tried to kill me and take my gold.
Lucy	Oh no. Not guns.
Sneer	I don't believe it. What sort of arms did they have?
Basil	The usual sort, you know, with hands on the end. [*GROAN!*]
Sneer	I meant firearms. What sort of guns?
Basil	Shot-guns. One was about to pull the trigger when the tin clattered at his feet and startled him. He looked round so I bopped him on the chin and he fell to the ground. Just then the other robber ran out at me with a pistol.
Lucy	How nasty.
Sneer	This is too bad to be true.
Basil	But all the tin tacks showered onto the

road right in front of the vicar on his bike. He swerved, burst a tyre and crashed into the second robber, knocking him out.

Lucy   Gosh.

Sneer   Blast!

Basil   So you see, I was saved. I want you to have this gold for saving my life.

Sneer   But it was me, do you hear me? I threw it out of the window. I saved your life. I want the reward. It's me you must thank.

Basil   I don't believe you. You're just a greedy, nasty little man. [CHEER!]

Lucy   The first thing I will do with the money is pay Sinbad Sneer his ten pence so he can go and never come back again.

Sneer   Darn it. I nearly got you. Blow!

Lucy   Now go away, leave me alone and never return.

Sneer   Oh very well. Bother it. [He goes] [CHEER!]

Basil   You're Lucy, aren't you?

Lucy   Yes. How did you know?

Basil   I have watched you every day at the

mill. You look even prettier in your new dress.

Lucy	Then who are you?
Basil	Basil. Basil Brimwick. My father owns the mill.
Lucy	So you're Mr Brimwick's son. How wonderful. You're the Basil all the girls talk about. You're the Basil who's so famous. You're the Basil who's so kind and strong and handsome.
Basil	That's right. That's the Basil. And you're the Lucy that I've been longing to meet. You're the girl I dream about.
Lucy	Oh, I say!
Basil	Don't say you're here all alone in this town with so many crooks about, ready to pounce on a poor young girl?
Lucy	I'm not all alone. I've got Bertie. But I don't think even he loves me any more. Today's my birthday, you see, and he's left me here by myself. [*AAH!*]
Basil	What a rotter! How could he leave such a pure white rose to wither on the heap?
Lucy	I beg your pardon?
Basil	Let me pick you and put you in a vase.

Lucy	You what?
Basil	I insist you let me take you out to dinner. Do you know of any good places to eat?
Lucy	The Queen's Arms? That's where Bertie will be.
Basil	Oh no – I know of hundreds of places better than there. Did you say The Queen's Arms?
Lucy	Yes.
Basil	I've just met a drunk chap from there. He dropped his bottle of gin as the vicar crashed his bike. He was coming this way.
Lucy	Surely not....
Basil	But I want to take you away from here. Oh let me, Lucy. How I want to look after you.
Lucy	Oh, Basil.
Basil	Oh, Lucy.
	[Bertie *bursts in – drunk*]
Bertie	Oh blimey!
Lucy	Bertie! You're drunk. Where have you been?

Bertie	The Queen's Arms. I bought some gin but I dropped the lot.
Basil	I'll see that you get some more.
Bertie	Who's this? I think I like him.
Lucy	Basil. I saved his life. He's going to take me out for a birthday treat. I think we've just fallen deeply in love. You don't mind or anything do you, Bertie?
Bertie	It's funny you should say that.
Basil	Now please don't take it too badly. It's just that Lucy and I have suddenly become very ... close.
Lucy	Very.
Bertie	And so have I.
Lucy	Pardon?
Basil	How do you mean?
Bertie	To the barmaid at The Queen's Arms. I've asked her to marry me. She said yes. [*CHEER!*]
Lucy	How super!
Basil	Splendid. Well done, old chap.
Bertie	She's got so much charm, so much warmth, and what is more ... so much gin.

Lucy	Oh Basil, things have worked out well after all.
Basil	And I want you to be my wife. Let's get the vicar downstairs.
Lucy	Why? He hasn't done us any harm.
Basil	To marry us, Lucy.
Lucy	Oh, Basil!
Bertie	Oh well, I'll be off then.
Basil	Let's all go out to celebrate.
Lucy	Oh yes, Basil, let's.
Basil	Just think – we're about to start a new life together. A new voyage. A journey over the sea through gentle waves to a distant shore....
Bertie	So you're going to Bognor for your honeymoon?
Basil	And I will now spend the rest of my life in your arms.
Lucy	And I, Basil my dear, will spend all my days in your arms.
Bertie	And I, with a bit of luck, will spend all mine in The Queen's Arms. Let's go. Cheers!

[*They exit to GROAN!*]